Planes, Trains and Chuck & Eddie
~A Lighthearted Look at Family

By Kerrie Flanagan

Printed in the United States of America

First Printing, 2013

Hot Chocolate Press

Cover design by Ania Cywińska

ISBN: 978-0-9910626-0-7

www.KerrieFlanagan.com

This book is dedicated to my family—all of my family: Drew, Delaney, Richard, the Stephens, the Senigs, the Flanagans, the Hultgrens, and the Vaughans. I am grateful to have all of you in my life.

A special thanks to my husband Rich for his continuous and loving support over the past 20+ years; I couldn't have done this without him.

Acknowledgments

The well-known proverb says it takes a village to raise a child; the same principle can be applied to a writer. It takes a whole village to help a writer learn the skills and build enough confidence to want to share her work with the world.

I have many people in my "village" I want to acknowledge, because without them, this project would have sat dormant on my computer.

First off, I am indebted to my amazing critique group. For 15 years, my Wednesday nights, from 7:00-10:00, have been devoted to Writer's Group where I have learned the horrors of passive voice, the subtleties of show don't tell and the importance of constructive criticism. But most of all, I learned the power of support and true friendship. To Ellen, Sally, Linda, Carol, Helen, LeAnn and Kelly, words can't express how grateful I am to have you all in my life.

To my writing buddies Laura and Dean, thank you for your help and support over the years with my writing and for your friendship.

April, thanks for the memories and all the wine. Beth, your friendship and support over the past two decades have meant the world to me. Cynthia, thanks for always pushing me to grow and expand my views through great books.

To all the current and past members of Northern Colorado Writers—thank you. You continually inspire me to keep moving forward with my writing.

Finally, a big thanks to my family. Mom and Dad your love, support and encouragement have been the strong foundation in my life, giving me the courage to pursue my dreams. Chuck and Eddie, regardless of what I said when you were born, I wouldn't trade you two for anything. You're the best brothers a woman could ask for. Rich, Drew and Delaney, thanks for always being there, for all the great laughs and for putting up with my craziness at times. I love you all!

Introduction

Family. Good or bad, “normal” or dysfunctional, we all have one. When we are young our family circle may include our parents, siblings and some extended family like grandparents, aunts and uncles. Then we grow up and many of us get married. This extends our circle to then include our spouse’s circle. Then siblings get married, bringing nieces and nephews, our own children get married and add grandchildren to the mix. Regardless of how it all plays out, our families grow as our life progresses.

Adding more people to the mix can make life messier and more unpredictable, but for me it also means more people in my circle: more people to visit on holidays, more people to have over for a barbeque and more people to create memories with.

This book of essays allows me a chance to share some of my favorite family memories and one rant related to parenting that I wrote in a moment of annoyance at something I read. Each essay stands on its own, so the order in which you read them doesn’t matter.

My hope is that as you read these not only do you enjoy the stories as written, but that they also draw out good memories of times with your own family.

~Kerrie

Table of Contents

Chuck and Eddie's Sister

—Living in the shadows

Growing up the older sister of twin brothers was not always easy—at times it was downright infuriating. I guess I even told my mom, after the boys were born and home for about a week, to take them back now.

My parents say I was an easy child. I smiled a lot, slept through the night and I breezed through the twos without an ounce of terribleness. When other parents would complain of sleepless nights or temper tantrums, my parents would listen but couldn't comprehend. My glory in the spotlight, and my mom and dad's skewed view of parenthood, ended after two and half years with the birth of my brothers, Chuck and Eddie.

Whatever my parents previously missed out on, they now experienced twofold: diapers, bottles, feedings, crying. Once my brothers were mobile and crawling around, it was hard for Mom and Dad to contain them. They tried using a baby gate, but the boys would have no part of that. One would hold the gate up while the other crawled under and then they would switch. As they grew into toddlerhood, the terrible twos became a harsh reality for my parents as my brothers embraced this stage with every bit of their being. When they were three they snuck over to a neighbor's house and ransacked their kitchen.

It became clear that my brothers were basically the anti-Kerrie. When I was asking people how I could help, my brothers were figuring out how to destroy everything in their path. From the moment they got out of bed in the morning, their energy ran at full throttle. Questions and chatter flowed out of them like a roaring river and drained all the life out of any adults within 50 feet.

As we grew up, the boys' reputations grew

too. When people found out who I was, a variety of reactions followed:

"You're Chuck and Eddie's sister?" the adults would say. Then they would shake their heads like they were talking to a widow at a funeral and say, "I'm sorry."

Others, usually young girls who liked the bad boy type, would squeal with delight, "You're Chuck and Eddie's sister?" Then they would reach out and longingly touch my arm as if by touching me that would somehow connect them to my brothers.

Then there were the older kids who would say through gritted teeth, "You're Chuck and Eddie's sister?" Some would even start hitting their hands with their fists.

Others would start shaking, "You're Chuck and Eddie's sister?" and suddenly become fidgety and keep looking over their shoulders.

Regardless of the reactions the end result remained the same. No matter what I did, I was known as Chuck and Eddie's sister. There was a time I wondered if I should legally change my name.

It felt like a spotlight followed them wherever they went and I was the stage manager in the background. Because I was a quiet and shy child, most of the time I was okay with it, but sometimes I felt like the little Whos from the Dr. Seuss story, *Horton Hears a Who*. They yelled from their city perched on a clover, "We are here!" at the top of their lungs in order to be noticed. I too was screaming, "I am here!" but for me it was quietly on the inside where no one heard.

As we entered our teen years, my brothers perfected their Chuck-and-Eddieness. They were now outgoing, handsome young men who thrived at being the life of any party and if you looked closely, you could see the mischievous glint in their green eyes as they calculated their next move.

We were three school years apart, so I never went to junior high or high school at the same time with them. I used this time to start coming out of my shell and begin to form my own identity.

Band and my friends were the reason I loved school. I played clarinet, cello and saxophone. In high school, marching band became my passion—my life. I eventually went on to become the drum major, leading our 180-piece band in many different competitions. My confidence grew and I was finally making a name for myself.

When the time came to step outside the nest and go off to college, I felt ready. A new phase in my life was about to begin and no one would know the names Chuck and Eddie. I would finally be free of that label.

Two weeks after settling into my dorm I got a call from childhood friend, Cindy. She and her family had lived two doors down from us until I was about 13 and then they moved away. Now, she lived in the same city as the college I attended. She heard I was in the area and called to invite me to a party. I hadn't seen her for years so I was excited to go.

When I arrived I saw one of her older brothers, Rich. He didn't notice me at first, but then I heard him ask who I was.

Cindy just looked at him and said loud enough for me to hear, "You know who she is."

He looked at me. "I have no idea who you are."

"Yes, you do." I smirked.

I could tell he was racking his brain to figure this out. "No, I really have no idea."

Before I could stop myself I blurted out a clue, "Chuck and Eddie."

He looked confused for a minute. Then it was like a light bulb went on and he smiled. "You're Chuck and Eddie's sister?"

I laughed and nodded my head.

I guess being Chuck and Eddie's sister isn't so bad after all because now Rich is Chuck and Eddie's brother (in law) and has been for the past 23 years.

The Gift

—Some of us have it, some of us don't

My husband, Rich, says he was born with it. He calls it The Gift. I've noticed other people, mostly men, possess this Gift as well. Personally, I do not belong to this elite group, and many times, I wish I did.

The Gift is the uncanny ability to tune out everything and everyone around you at a moment's notice. The perfect example is when my Rich is watching football on television. The children are playing all around him, yet he just sits there watching the game. He doesn't hear all the truck noises and singing. He just watches. Sometimes he reacts to the game, but is oblivious to the rest of the world. When the kids try to talk to him—nothing. It gets worse if they ask a question, because they expect a response. When they don't get one, they go off like some obnoxious car alarm:

Dad...Dad...Dad..Dad.Dad.Dad!!!!!!!!!!! The amazing thing is, he still doesn't notice them. I, on the other hand, can't take it anymore. I go over, shake him and tell him to answer the kids.

"What?" is the usual response.

Oh, how I wish I had The Gift. I often wonder what it is like to be in the world of The Gift. I bet it's quiet and serene like a country meadow in the summer. It has to be. Rich always has just the hint of a smile when he is in this world and he seems so content.

I keep hoping someday I will receive this wonderful Gift. I try to pretend I have it, but it doesn't take long to see I don't. I need it the most while driving in the car.

"Mom! He looks like he's going to touch me!"

"Mom! She made a face at me!"

At times like this, I don't enter into a calm country scene; I enter into a neurotic world. I start talking to myself. I keep telling myself if I just ignore them, they will stop.

"Mom! He's still looking at me!" I tell myself again to just ignore them, they will stop.

"Ow! Mom! She pinched me." Just ignore them... just ignore them...

"MMMOOOMMM!!"

I can't take it anymore! I pull the car over, turn around and yell something intelligent like, "I don't ever want to ever hear you say the word Mom again for the rest of your life!"

Although there appear to be many advantages, there is one down side to this Gift. I do not see the beauty in it when I am on the other side of it. I'll be pouring my heart out to my husband, telling him about some enlightening experience I just had. When I finish, I wait for some profound insight from him. All I get is the sound of crickets. Not a word. I usually scream and walk away.

Ah... The Gift. I dream about it. I wish for it. I often wonder if I can find it somewhere online. No luck so far though. Looking at the positive side, there must be a reason why I was not blessed with such a gift. Maybe I'm supposed to truly experience the world around me. You know, feel, empathize and definitely hear my children. Maybe I'm supposed to start a support group for people who live with The Gifted Ones. We can sit around and talk about how we are unlistened to and share stories to see who is living with the person with the biggest Gift.

I guess in the end, there's nothing I can do. We live in a world where some of us have it and some don't. It's not going to stop me from searching though. I will continue on my quest and someday, when you find me in front of the television watching Oprah, while the children are running all around, Rich is sitting next to me, pouring his heart out, and I just have the hint of a smile on my face, you will know I have finally found The Gift.

It's Not Windy Enough

—One little boy's dream to fly a kite

"Mommy, can we go fly my kite now?" These were the words I'd heard from my five-year-old son, Drew, every day for the past week. When I was young, I must have had a traumatic kite-flying experience, because I do not like to fly kites. So when Drew kept asking me if I would help him fly his kite, I used every excuse possible to avoid it. My most popular excuse was, it wasn't windy enough.

Well, this excuse was not going to work today. Today was one of those days that if you went outside to blow bubbles, all you would have to do is hold the wand out in the air and the wind would do all the work. I had no choice. I told him to go get his kite. Today was the day we would fly it. He ran to go get it before I could change my mind. I closed my eyes and tried to mentally prepare myself for this undertaking.

We went into the cul-de-sac to begin our adventure. I inhaled a deep breath of wind, hoping to build my confidence. He stood quietly and looked up at me with big blue eyes. I explained to him that I was going to throw the kite into the air while he held on to the string and ran down the street. The kite would go high in the air and we would have an incredible bonding experience.

Theoretically, I knew this would work. I asked him if he understood. He nodded. I handed him the string and I took the kite. I threw it in the air and he started running toward me. The kite came crashing down. So much for theories. I had him practice running down the street a few times and then we tried again. I threw the kite and he walked backward this time. The kite went up, but still came right back down.

I stared for a minute. Maybe it would be best if we switched jobs. Then I could get it flying and he could take over string control. This plan sounded much better than the first one. I explained my fool-proof plan to him. I gave him the kite, walked in the opposite direction to make the string tight and told him to let go. The kite went into the air. Success! I let more string out. It was still flying! I couldn't believe it. I let out more string. I was feeling quite proud.

"Come and hold the string," I yelled to Drew.

But it was too late. The kite string went loose and the kite started plummeting toward the ground. I panicked and ran down the street, yelling at the kite to stay up and looking over my shoulder every few steps to see if it was listening. (My neighbors must have thought I was being chased by a pack of wild animals.) It was no use; down came the kite and about half a block of string. Out of breath from my 50-yard dash, I stood at the end of the block, stared at Drew and thought, this is ridiculous. I'm getting too old for this. But... standing down there was a little boy who looked up to me. He had confidence in me. He thought I could really fly this thing. For him I would give it one more try.

I wanted to get back to him before I lost my nerve to try it again. Because of this, I didn't see any need to wind the string back up. After all, we would have to let it out again soon enough. So I headed back down the block, with a trail of string both in front of and behind me. The wind picked up and started to move the string all around me. I turned around, leaned over and grabbed the string behind me. I stood up and continued on. Somehow, though, the string got tangled around my shoes. I bent over and tried to undo it. A gust of wind blew some into my hair. When I stood up, I had string wrapped around my ankles, waist and head. I frantically tried to get myself out of this mess, all while I walked down the block. (If the neighbors didn't think I was crazy before, I was sure they did now.) By the time I reached Drew, I felt and looked like a helpless insect caught in a spider's web.

I peered at him through string-covered eyes. "Mommy is not very good with kites. You'll have to wait until Daddy gets home."

He didn't say anything. By the look on his face, I couldn't tell if he felt sorry for me or if he thought I was just pathetic. Either way, he didn't argue. He just turned around and went into the house.

I watched him go in. Thoughts raced through my mind: What kind of mother was I? I couldn't even fly a silly kite. I knew this would have some lasting effect on him. He probably would never ask me to do anything with him again. I began freeing myself from the web of kite string, but not from the guilt.

It then occurred to me that I was not a bad mother. I gave kite flying a try. I was being a good example! I knew going into it that I didn't like to fly kites and that I was not very good at it. But I did it anyway. I realized, I couldn't be good at everything. I knew what my strengths and weaknesses were. I knew what I had to work on (kite flying) and what skills I should be using to my full potential. I only hoped that next time he asked me to do something, I would get to utilize one of my strengths.

With a wad of string in one hand, a kite in the other and a new outlook on life, I went into the house. Standing there was Drew, dressed in full hockey gear and holding two hockey sticks in his hands. Through the black metal hockey mask I heard the words, "Mommy, will you play hockey with me?" I took a deep breath and thought, *here we go again.*

Soaring to New Heights

—Things you Don't Want to Hear from the Pilot

My husband Rich recently got his private pilot's license and we wanted to fly somewhere, just because we could. The idea of flying to another state in the morning and being back home a little after lunchtime sounded exciting and something out of the lives of the rich and famous.

So, we made plans to head to Sydney, Nebraska. Population: 9,000. Major industry: Cabela's—the premiere hunting, fishing and camping supply store.

Six a.m. came early on the morning of our adventure, especially for our children, 13-year-old Drew and 11-year-old Delaney. They weren't thrilled about getting up at the crack of dawn on a Saturday when teens and tweens were supposed to be sleeping in. Plus, Delaney was nervous about flying in a little four-seater plane and no matter how much I tried to convince her, Cabela's was not on her top ten list of must-visit shopping venues.

Sleepy-eyed and dazed we headed to the Fort Collins/Loveland airport. My excitement waned some when I saw the sky out east.

"Rich, do those clouds look okay over there?" I pointed toward the grayness.

"They look fine. No need to worry." He smiled but it did nothing to suppress my turbulent stomach.

We pulled the plane out of the hangar—literally hooked it up to the special airplane tow bar and pulled it out.

While Rich went through his preflight checklist, I studied the ominous-looking clouds to make sure they weren't getting darker. By the time all the final checks on the airplane were done my nerves were in a tailspin.

"Are you sure those clouds are—"

"We'll be fine," he said. "They're high enough, we won't even be getting near them."

"But what about thunderstorms? Or lightning hitting the plane? Or—"

He put his hand on my shoulder. "They're just gray clouds. There are no storms predicted. We'll be fine. Now get in the plane." He motioned toward the wing.

With Rich as pilot, Drew as co-pilot and Delaney and me in the small back seat, we all checked our seatbelts, put on our communication headphones and prepared for takeoff. I grabbed Delaney's hand, to help ease *her* nerves as we sped down the runway. I practiced some deep breathing of my own.

Soon the plane lifted off and we were flying!

Adrenaline surged through me as we went higher and higher. I slowly let go of her hand. We each looked out our window at the scene below. Matchbox-sized cars crawled along on the small highway. A farm with teeny tiny cows and houses that…

“Hey!” I yelled to Rich. “Quit hitting those bumps!” I grabbed Delaney’s hand again.

“I can’t help it,” he said. “They said there might be turbulence at 7,000 feet.”

My stomach lurched each time the plane did.

“I will go up to 9,000 feet to see if it’s better up there—oops.”

“Oops?” I said, surprised. “That is first on the list of ‘things you never want to hear your pilot say.’ No more oops.”

Rich just laughed. Drew laughed. Delaney and I huddled closer together to provide support through the bumpy climb to 9,000 feet. But as promised, the ride finally smoothed out and Rich set our course for Nebraska.

As the bumps subsided so did my grip on Delaney’s hand. Eventually we were both able to relax more and enjoy the rest of the flight.

“Look at all the circles on the ground,” said Delaney.

“Hey, look at that long train,” said Drew. “It looks like a toy.”

Although the scenery across the plains lacked diversity, seeing it from up in the air added intrigue.

The hour-long ride flew by and we soon saw the airport in the distance.

Rich called out, “Sydney traffic, this is one one eight foxtrot sierra. We are five miles west, inbound for runway.”

He waited and then repeated his call out. Nothing.

“Do they usually answer?” I asked.

“Yeah. They’re usually pretty talkative. Let me try again.”

Still, no response.

“That’s strange.”

“Um, strange how?” I asked. My stomach resumed its tightened state. “I don’t want to hear strange. That’s second on the list by the way. Can we still land?”

“Yeah, we can land. We just need to make sure there aren’t any other planes.”

Other planes?

Rich looked left, right, up. I did the same and so did the kids.

“Looks clear to me,” I said.

“Me too,” said Drew.

"Then it's time to land." Rich made adjustments on the control panel.

The plane angled down. I took a deep breath and my daughter's hand. The runway came closer and closer. Rich lined up and maneuvered the plane until it lightly touched down.

I exhaled, not realizing I had been holding my breath. "I give that landing a ten!"

"Thanks," said Rich.

"It was okay," said Drew.

"It was good, Dad." Delaney smiled.

We taxied up to the small airport, passing one other plane, and found a place to park.

It felt good to get out and stretch my legs. We helped Rich tie down the plane and went into the nearby building. Paneling covered the walls and the smell of stale coffee filled the air.

A voice from a small room behind the counter said, "I heard your callout all three times. I answered, but you must not've heard me."

I peeked in the room and a man in a flannel shirt and baseball cap sat at a desk with a microphone and some other electronic devices on it.

"I wonder what happened?" Rich said.

After some small talk with the airport guys, the Cabela's shuttle arrived and took us to our final destination.

We entered the 85,000-square-foot store and stood there in awe. Drew, who loves anything camouflage, must have thought he had died and gone to heaven. An invisible force pulled him into the sea of green, brown and tan merchandise before us and he soon disappeared.

Delaney, Rich and I still hadn't moved. We all stared at the display at the very back of the store. There were mountain goats, moose, elk, deer and even an elephant. The good thing was, they weren't moving.

"Okay," I broke the silence. "Let's see what's here."

For an hour we wandered around checking out the wares and immersing ourselves in the full Cabela's experience. There was a General Store, clothing and gear for every outdoor activity imaginable and lots of camping gadgets. We passed some time watching the big fish in the gigantic tank. Drew emerged from the camouflage and we ate lunch at the small café before catching the shuttle back to the airport with our treasures: fudge, jerky spices, candy and a camouflage hat (a gift for Drew).

Back at the airport we loaded us and our stuff into the plane.

Rich adjusted the dials. "Oh, here's the problem." He laughed. "I didn't have the volume turned up. That's why we couldn't hear the airport dispatcher."

I just shook my head. With all the final checks done, we took off into the dreary sky and flew toward home. I knew we were safe with Rich as pilot so the dark clouds didn't even bother me now. I didn't even need to hold Delaney's hand anymore to make *her* feel better. She wanted to look out the window at the scenery.

The plane leveled off and it was smooth flying from there. I never have a problem sleeping in the car, so I am sure it was no surprise to my family when the hum and movement of the plane soon lulled me to sleep.

I woke up when we were about 10 minutes away from the local airport when the ride went from very smooth to very bumpy.

Rich called the airport. This time we heard their response and when we were clear to land, we began our descent. The plane jostled us around.

"This wind is crazy," Rich commented.

We flew over the highway, circled around and lined up for the runway. The plane lurched left and right.

"Geez, Rich, aren't we supposed to go in straight?"

"It's the wind," he said. "I've never landed in wind this strong before."

"That's third on the list, Rich." I grabbed Delaney's hand and started my deep breaths.

With the plane at a tilt, Rich began the descent. As the ground neared, my insides jostled around in sync with the plane. Closer and closer, then the wheels slammed on the runway, bounced up and came back down on one, back up and then both wheels settled on the ground. I let go of Delaney's hand.

"That was awesome!" said Drew.

"I give that landing a six," I told him.

"A six! You have no idea how hard that landing was."

"Sorry, but I call them as I feel them," I said.

He taxied the plane toward the hangar.

"Well, if it makes you feel any better, Dear, I do give our whole trip a ten!"

"Me too!" said Delaney.

It's Not My Fault!

-What were they thinking?

Just when I think our world cannot get any crazier I pick up the newspaper and see the headline, "Activists blame obesity on sugary SpongeBob." SpongeBob causes childhood obesity? Apparently the Center for Science in the Public Interest and the Campaign for a Commercial-Free Childhood are threatening to sue Viacom (owner of Nickelodeon) unless it takes SpongeBob off sugary, unhealthy snacks. I guess having cartoon characters' images on junk food boxes has some profound effect on people's good judgment.

Here I was, the whole time thinking it was the consumption of junk food and lack of exercise that causes childhood obesity. The good thing is now I can rest easy knowing it is not my fault if my kids get fat. It's Viacom's fault for putting images of my favorite Bikini Bottom resident on a box of food. What a relief! I no longer have to accept any responsibility for my choices. Without any guilt or remorse, I can succumb to my young cherubs' pleas of "Mommy, can we get that?!" and load up my grocery cart with Pop-Tarts, Cheez-Its, Fruit Roll-Ups and sugary cereals all with cartoon characters on the packaging. Then I can let my offspring gorge themselves until their bellies are nice and round and rest assured that I had nothing to do with their unhealthy eating habits. Once again the trend in this country continues—blame everyone else when we make stupid choices.

One of the parents brainwashed into joining this sweet crusade claims that the irresponsible marketing to young children undermines her efforts as a parent. She claims she does her best to have her kids eat healthy food but with all those enticing junk food ads on television and the cartoon characters on junky snacks and cereals it just makes her job as a mom difficult and it must be stopped.

No one ever said parenting is easy, but threatening to sue a company is not the answer. I think this woman needs to follow David Spade's example on the Capital One commercials: "No. No. Uh, nope. Nooo." Or she can turn off the television so her little sugar puffs don't watch the commercials, get a DVR system so they can fast-forward through the commercials or she doesn't have to take the kids to the grocery store. There are so many other options but in our lawsuit-happy society, there are lawyers ready to gather a posse of "victims" who don't have a backbone or enough sense to make a good decision. The lawyers play on all those little insecurities all parents have regarding whether or not they are doing what is best for their child. They convince these parents that it isn't their fault their children are starting to look like the Pillsbury Doughboy, but it's those awful companies preying on our kids. When the troops are successfully rallied, they all pounce on unsuspecting businesses and threaten a lawsuit.

I really could care less that SpongeBob's face is on a box of cereal, but I am concerned about these parents and the message they are teaching children.

With this silly lawsuit, the clear message is that people do not have the power over what they buy and how they spend their money. The media holds all the power. If people eat too much, drink too much, buy too much… it is the media's fault because people watched and believed the commercials that told them they needed to have something, that their life would not be complete without it. Somewhere along the way these parents formed the idea that they just don't have the ability to refrain from all that temptation. What a scary thought.

Maybe I can sue this group because they are undermining MY efforts as a parent. They are showing my children we do not have the power to make our own decisions. And because of that, we do not have to accept the outcomes of our choices. When things turn out badly, it is always someone else's fault. I could sue these people because I am sure there is a lawyer out there willing to help me. But the bottom line is, I would rather put all that time and effort into actually being a good role model for my kids and teaching them there are consequences for our choices—both good and bad.

Pizza Alley

—A beacon of light in a dark pizza world

Back in the summer of 1975, when I was almost seven years old and my brothers Chuck and Eddie were four, my parents decided it was time to head west. If it was good enough for the Pioneers, it was good enough for us. While packing up the house, Mom played her John Denver album over and over. By the time we said our good-byes to grandparents, aunts, uncles and cousins, my brothers and I knew every word to "Rocky Mountain High." We left Long Island behind and traveled to Colorado where my mom's brother and a cousin had already moved.

We settled in a suburb outside of Denver. We all loved the mountains, especially my mom, and we adjusted pretty quickly to calling soda "pop" and referring to our sneakers as "tennis shoes." But the biggest culture shock for my parents was the food. Colorado did not have a high Jewish population, so finding good bagels and a kosher deli was like trying to find good Mexican food in New York. Mom always complained that there were no good bakeries, in fact there were no bakeries at all and my dad suffered from severe pizza withdrawal.

It's not like Colorado didn't have pizza, but we quickly learned there was a difference between Colorado and New York pizza—a big difference. Our first western pizza experience happened at a place called Shaky's. This precursor to Chuck E. Cheese had arcade games scattered throughout and to liven the place up, a banjo player provided the music. Dad, a professional guitar player, had only two instruments he loathed: one was the bagpipes and the other was the banjo. So, for my dad, this was an instant strike against the establishment.

Regardless of the *Deliverance* ambiance, we stayed, hoping the pizza would save us. My brothers, who never sat still, immediately badgered Mom and Dad for quarters for the arcade games. Dad dug to the depths of his pockets and Mom to the bottom of her purse. The more quarters they could find, the more peace it would bring them. They handed their offering to Chuck and Eddie knowing it wouldn't last long and ordered the pizza. I was content to sit at the table and wait.

It wasn't long before the boys returned full force.

"Mom, can I have more quarters? Can I?" Chuck jumped up and down. "There's this one game that I really like. Mom? Do you have any quarters?"

Eddie went straight to Dad. "Do you have any quarters, Dad? I want to play that one game over there again. Dad?"

Thankfully the pizza arrived. Food always had the power to quiet my brothers, even if only for a short time.

"Sit down, boys," Mom said.

They sat and we all looked at the pizza.

"Maybe it tastes better than it looks," Dad joked.

Mom picked up a slice and tried to fold it in half (like all New Yorkers do). It snapped. She dropped it like it had some contagious disease and spewed a string of expletives we were used to hearing. Mom could hold her own in a roomful of sailors.

Dad cautiously took a bite and by the look on his face, you would have thought he just bit into a lemon. He dropped his piece back onto the plate. “This isn’t pizza. This is cardboard with cheese. I can’t eat this.”

I tried it and because I really only had about four years of pizza-eating experience behind me, I didn’t really mind. My brothers had already each finished one piece and were working on their seconds, but their opinion didn’t count at all. They would eat anything. When they were two, I caught them sitting on the kitchen floor with a bag of dog food between them, eating it like it was cereal.

We waited for the boys to finish and then left. My parents, clearly disgusted, vowed to never inflict bad Colorado pizza on us again. And thus my dad’s quest for good pizza began.

***

After months of searching and a few close calls, Dad announced that his quest was over. He found the Holy Grail: a pizza place owned by a guy from Brooklyn. We loaded into the VW Bus and drove the 30 minutes to Pizza Alley.

On the outside, it wasn't anything spectacular—a small building with a glass storefront and we could see about 10 small tables. But when we went in, you would have thought my parents had just passed the Pearly Gates in Heaven.

Mom stopped and inhaled the aroma. "Ed, you may have found it." She pointed behind the counter. "Look, they even have real pizza ovens."

The guy behind the counter looked at Dad. "How ya doin'? What can I get ya?"

He sounded like our relatives back east. The other guy next to him tossed the flat pizza dough into the air and caught it. My brothers ran over to where he was to get a closer look and to start their usual string of questions that they really didn't want the answer to—they just liked hearing themselves talk.

Dad smiled. “One large cheese for here and five sodas.”

We all sat down at a table that was covered with a red and white checkered table cloth. Mom and Dad were like kids at Christmas. They smiled and reminisced about the pizza places of their youth and my brothers’ nonstop chatter and bounciness didn’t even faze them.

The pizza and the moment of truth arrived. We all watched as Mom took a piece and folded it in half. She grinned. The end part of the slice flopped a little and grease dripped onto the paper plate.

“Oh, Ed, this looks perfect.”

She took a bite and savored it before releasing a string of expletives, but this time they were all good.

Dad took a slice, properly folded it and took a bite. He seemed to be having an out of body experience.

After taking another bite, Mom gave us each a slice. “Now this is real pizza, kids. This is what pizza is supposed to be like.” She handed it to us like it was pure gold.

***

Trips to Pizza Alley soon became a regular part of our lives. Whenever Mom and Dad were craving pizza, which was at least once a month, we loaded into the green Nova and drove 30 minutes to the little piece of New York dropped into Denver. We all enjoyed these outings because it meant time together as a whole family. Dad worked a 9-5 job at Blue Cross and Blue Shield and then on many evenings he had gigs playing his guitar, so getting to do something all together was great. My brothers' incessant talking and lack of awareness for others' personal space didn't bother me as much on Pizza Alley nights.

This went on for years and during that time my brothers and I were being primed to be East Coast pizza aficionados. This was a time before Dominos became too popular, so Mom and Dad were able to shield us from the horrors of Colorado pizza. It became engrained, deep within us, what real pizza looked, smelled and tasted like.

One fateful fall evening, we loaded into the Chevy Vega. Mom made me sit in between Chuck and Eddie because they had been driving her crazy all afternoon. This was not a good sign because the boys were usually better behaved on Pizza Alley nights and I hated the job of human buffer zone. In the '70s nobody wore seatbelts, so the backseat of a car could become a war zone.

As we neared our destination, Mom and Dad's gasp interrupted the boys trying to hit each other around me in the back seat. Chuck and Eddie stopped and we all looked out the front window. We couldn't believe our eyes. Dad pulled into the parking lot, we all got out and stood there in a line, staring at what used to be Pizza Alley. Now it was burnt remnants of a building. A building that linked us to our past lives 1,800 miles away. A building that had become an extension of our family and the only place we knew where to get REAL pizza. If this were a scene in a movie, my parents would have fallen to their knees and cursed the heavens, screaming, "How could you let this happen?!"

But this wasn't the movies. Instead, my mom just cursed and we all got back into the car. The 30-minute ride home was silent.

We all mourned the loss of our beloved Pizza Alley, but Dad was hit the hardest by it. His determination to find good pizza remained intact for a few months, but then it began to wane when his searches came up empty. Eventually he resigned himself to the fact that we were doomed to eat Colorado pizza for the rest of our lives and he lowered his standards in order to fulfill his craving. But all of us continued to search for another oasis in this western pizza desert.

***

It has been 34 years since we lost Pizza Alley. Over the decades, more and more food comforts from the east infiltrated Colorado. We found good bagel places, occasionally Mom and Dad came across a Kosher deli and more decent pizza places popped up. My brothers and I are all married and have families now, but I have always been on a quest to reconnect with my childhood and my roots.

One summer afternoon, Mom and Dad made the 30-minute drive to our house for a visit. I had a big surprise for them when they arrived.

"Mom, Dad, you know all the restaurants and stores that have been built behind us?"

They nodded, not sure where this conversation was going.

"Well, there's a pizza place and I think you're going to like it. Plus we can walk there from here."

"Really?" Mom seemed to be getting excited.

"Are you sure it's good?" Dad didn't seem to want to get his hopes up.

I laughed. "I'm sure. I have been trained by the best."

The minute we walked into the restaurant, Mom stopped to inhale the almost forgotten aromas. My parents watched the dough being tossed into the air and saw that the pizza was sold by the slice and they smiled. We ordered a large cheese and sodas.

When the pizza arrived, the scene from our first visit to Pizza Alley replayed in my mind and in front of me.

I watched as Mom took a piece and folded it in half. She grinned. The end part of the slice flopped a little and grease dripped onto the paper plate.

"Oh, Kerrie, this looks perfect."

She took a bite and savored it before releasing a more refined string of expletives that indicated she was ecstatic.

Dad took a slice, properly folded it and took a bite. From the look on his face, I had a feeling I had found our new Pizza Alley.

***

Three weeks later I called my parents.

"Hey, Mom, do you guys want to join us at the new pizza place for dinner tonight?"

She laughed. "We would love to, except that we were just there last night. Maybe next time?"

The Birth of Our Remodel

—Sometimes change is good

I don't remember the exact moment of conception, but I do remember how I felt when Rich and I finally decided it was time to remodel and add an addition onto our 10-year-old house. We were both thrilled! Like expectant parents, we glowed and shared the news with everyone. I read as many books on the subject as I could, talked with people and prepared myself for the big event.

My husband, a drywall contractor, was overseeing the whole project, so I knew we were in good hands. I sat and dreamed of my new house. The colors I wanted. The artwork. The furniture. I couldn't wait to experience the birth of our "new" house. Ahhhh. It was sheer bliss.

With summer approaching, we started the whole process by adding a new office for me on the main floor where the living room used to be and remodeled three of the four bedrooms upstairs. We tore down and moved walls, painted walls and rearranged furniture. After two weeks, we settled the kids into their freshly painted bedrooms.

New carpet, lush green paint on the walls, book shelves and a comfy reading chair gave my office a warm, inviting feeling. The French doors created a sense of importance and a way to temporarily close out the rest of the world while I worked. I was elated. This room was going to be the perfect place to be productive, but also a place to relax.

The satisfying feeling of accomplishment lasted for about 1.5 days before the first wave of nausea hit.

It was time to get to work on the rest of the house where every room was being remodeled and a 600 square foot addition was being added. Everything we didn't need was boxed up and piled from floor to ceiling in the garage. Then we stacked all the furniture wherever it would fit: our bedroom, the garage and my newly remodeled office. Now instead of looking out the beautiful bay window to see the trees and blue sky while I worked at my desk, I saw brown leather recliners stacked two high, the back of the big screen television and boxes. Lots of boxes. There would be no relaxing here.

I looked around and my stomach tightened up. I wondered what I had gotten myself into.

The "morning sickness" surged again when we ripped up the carpet, the linoleum and the baseboard trim. Unneeded walls were beaten down. Then we headed outside to pull the siding off the back of the house. I nibbled on saltine crackers and sipped ginger tea to settle my stomach, but to no avail.

Moments of excitement periodically surfaced, like the day we recruited the neighbors to raise the walls of the addition. I patted the big dirt pile in the backyard and smiled as two-by-fours began to create the structure. It looked like an ultrasound picture of a developing baby. I could now see the skeleton and it gave me new hope and even some strength.

But on this rollercoaster ride, my strength soon waned when I sent Drew and Delaney off to start school again and I was left alone, in the big empty, dusty, quiet house. Well, not really quiet or alone because someone was always banging, sawing or drilling, which made working from home a nightmare.

The months dragged on and it became a pain to clear off the inch of dust in the kitchen every evening before preparing dinner. But as the leaves outside began to turn colors and die, my house began to come to life. Electrical wires now ran through the framing, ductwork was installed and new walls enclosed it all. As we approached the "due date," we were excited about our new house but everyone was on edge and irritability reached new heights. I cried at the drop of a hammer and snapped at Rich and the kids over things like chewing their food too loudly.

The four of us craved normalcy again. We were tired of cramming onto the one futon in the new loft to watch television in the evening. We were tired of the dust. We were tired of the noise. We were just plain tired. The urge to quit weighed heavy, but the urge to have our house back was stronger so we pushed ahead.

Eight months passed and Christmas loomed around the corner, as did the two parties I naively planned to have at our house. I looked around at the freshly painted walls, the new bamboo floor and the new carpet. Clearly, the due date neared, but some final projects like countertops and cupboards still needed to be finished and I was exhausted. I reached the point where I didn't care how much it would cost or how it was going to happen, I just wanted it done.

One day while the kids were off at school, Rich found me in my office with my head on my desk. "It's time," he said.

"Now?" I whined.

"Yes, now. It's time to put everything away."

"But I'm too tired."

He looked at me. "I need you to stay focused. We need to push through this and we will be done."

I forced myself out of my chair and together we went to tackle the mounds of boxes in the garage. One by one we unpacked our forgotten treasures and put them away. After hours of strenuous labor, the pile disappeared.

"We're almost done," he said. "Let's get the furniture."

"I can't do this anymore!" I cried.

"Yes, you can. Just think about how you'll feel when this is over. Let's go."

We tackled the stacks of furniture in my office.

"Uggg. This is heavy," I said.

"Just keep breathing," Rich said, unfazed.

"Hee. Hee. Hee." I panted.

Piece by piece we moved the leather recliners and sectional into place.

"Last one!" said Rich.

"Hee. Hee. Hee." I continued.

Through the kitchen, down the stairs and into the family room we went.

"Let's put it over here," Rich instructed. "Come on, push!"

"I am!" I said between breaths. Sweat beaded on my forehead.

One last big push and it was done.

I collapsed on the loveseat and caught my breath. I looked around at my new home and smiled.

"We did it, Rich."

"Yes, we did," he smiled back.

Our new home was born.

After resting and admiring our new addition, I regained my energy and my excitement. I got up and skimmed my fingers over the freshly painted walls, played with the new lights and walked barefoot on the new carpet. When the kids came home from school, they ran around checking out everything, grateful to have more living space again.

Excited to show off the fruits of our labor, I sent out the announcements for the two holiday parties. For each one Rich and I cleaned the house and dressed it up with fresh flowers.

Like any proud mother, I soaked in all the "ooh's" and "ahh's" as friends and family arrived and I graciously accepted the compliments.

"This is beautiful."

"Love the colors."

"I bet you are glad this is done."

"It's so warm and inviting."

After the final guests left, Rich and the kids and I took off our shoes and spread out on our theater-style recliners in our new family room to watch the big screen television.

Still reveling in the post-party excitement, I looked around.

"You know, Rich, now that all the hard work is done, I realize it wasn't that bad after all." I smiled. "Maybe in a couple years, we can think about adding a sunroom."

Before

After

Bucket List

—Dreams do come true

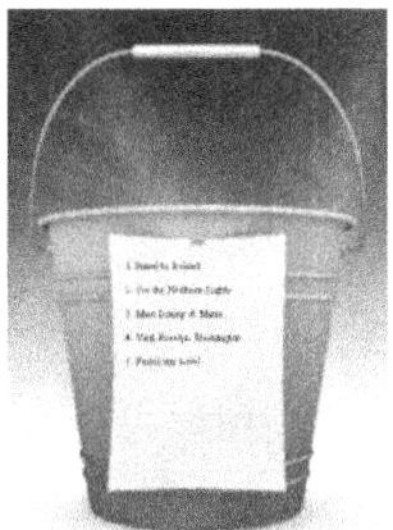

Rich strolled into my home office and handed me an envelope. “Here, happy early birthday.”

“Really?” I love surprises and this definitely counted for two reasons: one, my birthday was still a few weeks away and two, because birthdays were never high on my husband’s priority list. I often wondered if they were even stored in his memory at all.

I opened the envelope, took out the papers. My eyes skimmed the page then stopped. Las Vegas.

“We’re going to Vegas?” I stood up from my chair. He grinned. “Yes, we are going to Vegas.”

I wrapped my arms around him. “Thank you! When are we leaving? Where are we staying? How long are we there for?”

“Keep reading.”

I let go of him. “Okay, okay.” My hands trembled and my face hurt from smiling. I found the dates, the hotel and then went to the next page. I gasped, looked at him, then looked back down at the page. “Is this for real?”

“Yes.” He let out a small laugh.

I stared at him. “You got us tickets to see Donny and Marie?”

“Yes.”

I let out a scream. “We’re going to see Donny and Marie? Oh my God. Really?” I jumped up and down. “This is going to be the best birthday ever!” I gave him another hug. Looked at the paper. Gave him another hug and sat down. I exhaled. I was going to see Donny and Marie. I jumped up and gave him one more hug just in case he missed the other ones.

This duo had been part of my life since I was eight years old. Their television variety show captured my attention every week. I wasn’t sure if I was a little bit country or a little bit rock and roll, but it didn't matter. I never missed an episode if I could help it. The week Donny was on *The Love Boat* I cleared my busy elementary school calendar to make sure I was home to watch it and I wasn't disappointed.

Over the years I followed their careers and lives. I was not a fanatic about it. I couldn't name all of Donny's five boys or Marie's eight children, I didn't own all their albums/CDs and I didn't know their birthdays (I take that back, I did learn that Marie turned 50 on October 13, a few weeks after our trip).

For some reason they have always fascinated me. I read Donny's memoir, *Life Is Just What You Make It: My Story So Far*, and I looked forward to reading Marie's, *Might As Well Laugh About It Now*. One of my favorite movies and soundtracks is *Joseph and the Amazing Technicolor Dreamcoat* starring Donny. I melt every time I hear him sing. I even voted for Marie each week she was on *Dancing with the Stars* and I did the same for Donny when he was on it.

I remember one time, my daughter Delaney and I were watching television and a commercial came on announcing that the whole Osmond clan was going to be on Oprah. I screamed, making her jump. Once she recovered, she glared at me and then rolled her eyes, clearly not getting the incredibleness of this event. I recorded the episode on the DVR and watched it over and over.

Bottom line is (this is absolutely true), they were on my Bucket List of people to meet before I died.

Now I was going to see them in person (insert another scream) and I felt like a kid all over again. My dilemma was that I needed to figure out how to meet them and not just see the concert (since they were on my list). My husband didn't see the need to pay the extra $250 for the VIP tickets, even though it also included a photo op and he knew how much I loved Donny and Marie.

I put a call out on my blog, asking my readers for their ideas on how I could meet my favorite duo. The suggestions came rolling in, from faking press credentials, to creating a made-up award to present to them back stage, to calling Oprah to ask her to pull some strings.

The one suggestion that seemed the easiest to do was to round up the money and upgrade my regular tickets to the VIP ones, which included a meet and greet afterward. My parents graciously stepped up and offered to pay for the upgrade (actually, they were probably tired of my whining). I thought I was home-free.

Not so. Because Rich bought the tickets through an outside vendor, the Flamingo wouldn't upgrade the seats and the other vendor didn't sell the VIP seats. I talked, begged and pleaded with four different people, but no luck. The only thing they said I could do was check in with the box office the day of the show and if there were still VIP tickets available, I could upgrade then. Disappointed, I resigned myself to the fact that I was going to have to be patient and wait until the day of the show to see what I could do.

Then I thought about the other suggestions people made. I am not good at lying or at stretching the truth so the ideas of faking an award or press credentials were clever, but I knew I wouldn't be able to do it. I'd be a mess.

But I do have writing credentials, so I thought about combining that fact with openly disclosing that

I am a big fan. Now I needed to find the right person to talk to.

I tracked down Donny's manager and Marie's publicist and sent them both an email explaining that I was a huge fan and coming to see the show that week. I also said that as a freelance writer, I was always looking for article ideas (which is so very true). I went on to explain the ideas I had, included a list of my published clips and asked for a 15-minute interview.

We headed to Las Vegas before I heard an answer, but I packed my computer in order to be ready. Once there, I tried really hard not to be compulsive about checking for a reply and my patience paid off. The second morning of our trip I checked and there in the inbox was a reply from Marie's publicist. I closed my eyes and opened it.

"Please, please, please make this work," I whispered.

Her response read:

Hi Kerrie –

Unfortunately an interview will not be possible due to their schedules. I hope you enjoy the show.
Best, Ann

Damn.

It was now back to plan A—a true test of my patience. I would have to wait 48 hours until the day of the show to see if I could add the meet and greet onto my ticket.

When the countdown clock hit zero, we headed to the box office where I told the tattooed ticket guy behind the counter that I wanted to buy a VIP ticket.

"Sorry, the show is all sold out," he said, "and there are no more VIP tickets available."

"What? You're kidding." I shook my head. "I can't believe this."

Sorry was all he could say.

"All I want to do is meet them after." I looked at Rich. "This stinks." I took a deep breath.

"Oh," said Tattoo Man. "If all you want to do is meet them, let me see if I can add that." He punched some keys on the computer. "Your seat will still be the same though."

"I don't care," I said, getting a little excited.

"Okay." He typed some more and then handed me a VIP ticket for after the show. Woo hoo! I couldn't believe it.

The night of the show arrived and my insides were spinning faster than a slot machine. I got a special VIP badge and an 8 x 10 photo of each of them before going to our seats. My head reeled. This was it. I was going to meet Donny and Marie. The show itself was amazing and had all the bells and whistles you would expect in a Vegas show. There was singing, dancing, jokes and more singing. The highlight for me was when Marie sang an opera number. It was fantastic.

As the show neared an end my nerves were on overdrive. This was really happening. Donny and Marie gave a final wave, "goodnight, everybody," and left the stage.

Rich couldn't go with me so I said I would call him when it was over. I was ushered to a holding area where I stood in line with all the other fans waiting to meet the famous duo. I felt like Ralphie from *Christmas Story* when he was waiting in line to see Santa. As the line trudged along, I thought of all the questions I wanted to ask—all the profound things I wanted to say.

I watched as the people before me had their moment with Donny and Marie and with each step closer, my knees felt weaker and the knot in my stomach tightened. Four people in front of me, three, two… Then it was my turn. I was ushered over to Donny first. He was just as handsome (if not more so) in person. I introduced myself, gave him a hug and then all coherent thoughts vanished from my brain. Just like Ralphie when he finally got to sit on Santa's lap and Santa asked him what he wanted for Christmas. All he could do was stare at him. That was me. All I could do was stare at Donny and smile. He asked where I was from and I think I said Colorado, but I am not entirely sure. After that it was all a blur.

Then I was instructed to turn around for the photo (imagine the Christmas elves with Ralphie, moving him around, only these "elves" were nice). Marie came up and we took the photo. Then I faced Marie (who is also gorgeous up close) and my moment with Donny was over. Where did all my questions go? What about all the deep and profound things I wanted to say?

My brain finally started to reboot and at least I got in a few comments and questions for Marie. I told her I was a writer, I said my husband brought me here for my birthday and I that I was looking forward to reading her book. I started to relax a little, then the Donny and Marie "elves" tapped me on my shoulder signaling my turn was over.

This can't be, I thought. I had only been here for a couple of minutes. Everyone else got to talk to them longer. When that didn't work, they gently took my arm and guided me away. I tried to pull away, but the elves were stronger.

Once they let go of me I thought of running back to give Donny and Marie another hug or yell something memorable as I walked away like, "I have been fans of you guys forever and I love your music and I think you inspire many people and Donny if something ever happens to your wife, call me!" but I didn't. I just walked away, a smile on my face and my bucket now full.

From Princesses to Pirates

—Riding out the storm

The day my brother Eddie and his wife Heather became foster parents to two-and-a-half-year-old twins, Damian and Darian, their “ship” changed course and all they could do was hold on for the ride.

For 10 years their home had been filled with princesses, ponytails and politeness. As the parents of four girls ranging in age from 3 to 10, Eddie and Heather felt they had everything under control.

They had a good understanding of what girls were all about. As the one male in this world of princesses, Eddie was great at fitting in and was the knight in shining armor in this pink fairy-tale world.

He attended more tea parties than he'd ever admit to his friends and he could put the girls' hair in ponytails faster than you could say "Barbie."

Manners were important and instilled in the girls early on. Pleases and thank yous filled their home. Hair ties, barrettes and frilly hats covered the bathroom counter. When they took the family out to dinner, they often received compliments regarding the girls' good behavior.

Around age three, each of the girls went through their princess stage. They dressed up in the pinkest, shiniest, laciest clothes they could find and slipped into some oversized heels. The linoleum kitchen floor became their runway.

"Mommy, look at my fabulous dress," they would say to Heather while sauntering across the room. This phase in their lives was all about looking good and being sure to accessorize properly.

Playtime was organized with rules and lots of discussion. It didn't matter if the girls were playing ball outside or playing a game inside, whatever they did, there always seemed to be some level of control.

Don't get me wrong, it wasn't always tea parties and rainbows for them. The girls had their share of arguments, screaming matches and even the occasional tantrums. Just the fact there were four of them meant activity always filled their house. But when it came time to relax, the girls had no problem sitting and reading a book, coloring or watching a movie.

Life was pretty predictable for Eddie, Heather and the girls. That was until two little pirates, Damian and Darian, clamored onboard their family ship. Adorable, with sweet smiles, they overflowed with the true essence of two-year-olds and boyhood. They were energetic, curious, fearless and constantly on the move.

Their calm princess ship was rocked to the core. They had to batten down the hatches, revise their course of action and prepare for the journey ahead. Any sense of direction and predictability was immediately thrown overboard.

As foster children, the boys had more than your typical two-year-old issues. Their first two years of life were filled with uncertainty, inconsistency, many changes and limited boundaries. To them everything was fair game to touch, taste and ultimately destroy.

The noise level in their house went from chatty to thunderous upon the boys' arrival. Gone were the days of all the kids sitting down reading a book. The boys would have no part of it—they had a whole world to conquer.

And conquer they did. Sticks became swords, spoons became guns, stairs became slides. They were oblivious to the potential consequences of their actions. It seemed their motto was "smile and go for it!"

Heather spent her days trying to keep them safe and alive. While one of the boys slid down the banister, the other bolted for the front door. She would have to make a mad dash for the banister boy and yell at one of the older girls to nab the other one. After rounding them up and bringing them to what she thought was a safe location, she would try to take a moment to recover.

One of the girls would sashay up to her. "Mommy, look at my sparkly purple dress."

"Oh, that is beautiful honey. Turn around, let me—"

Another girl would run up. “Mommy, Darian is eating something from the trash and I don’t know what it is.”

Heather would stop him, just in time to see Damian taking off the plastic safety cover from the outlet, getting ready to stick something into it. By the time Eddie came home from work each night, Heather looked liked she had been fed to the sharks.

Every day they felt as if their ship traveled through a big storm with waves crashing against it, wind howling, no direction and all they could do was hang on. By the evening the storm would subside and their crew would go to sleep. Then it would be morning again, and “all hands on deck!”

This went on for several long months. Just as Eddie and Heather were at the end of their rope, something amazing started to happen. The storms became rain showers, then just overcast, then the sun started to appear more often and their ship became more steady.

Their pirates began learning from the princesses. There were more pleases and thank yous, they would sit for a few minutes to hear a story and occasionally you could spot a pirate running around in a pink, sparkly skirt.

Their princesses began learning that not everything had to begin with a plan and discussion. Sometimes it was just fun to let loose, jump in and try something new. Plus, pirates have some great toys to play with.

Damian and Darian did not arrive into their lives the same ways the girls did, but that doesn't matter. With the adoptions of the boys finalized, their permanent crew is now complete. Eddie and Heather don't always know the direction they are going, but with all their princesses and pirates onboard, they are excited about the adventure that lies ahead.

The Games People Play

—All in good fun

Growing up, we didn't really play games much as a family. We had a few board games, but if all the pieces were there, it was pretty amazing. Outside, our croquet set sometimes made an appearance at summer family parties and on rare occasions my dad played what he called "running bases" with us. It was like pickle, where two people threw a ball back and forth and everyone else ran between the two bases trying not to get tagged.

Toward the end of my elementary school years my grandma moved to Colorado and she played more games with us, but her game of choice was penny poker. She brought over a jar of pennies and her cards and taught us the ins and outs of Five-Card Draw, Seven Card Stud and Follow the Queen. Any money we won, we could keep, which on a good day was at least 50 cents.

But even though we didn't play games much, we did other things together as a family. Many nights after dinner, my brothers and I crammed onto the small piano bench by the baby grand piano in our living room. Mom cleaned up from our meal and Dad had the job of keeping us occupied and out of her way.

We sang songs I'm not sure were in the repertoire of most children. "Yellow Submarine," "Octopus's Garden" and "Joy to the World" (the Three Dog Night, Jeremiah was a bullfrog one) were some of our favorites and we also made up our own songs like "The Jello Kids" and "Lincoln Tunnel."

For my first seven years of life, we lived in New York before moving to Denver. After less than a year of living in Denver, my parents moved us all to Northglenn, a suburb about 20 minutes from the capital city. I was going into third grade and my brothers into kindergarten. Within ten minutes of being at our new house, my never-shy brothers found the other kids in the neighborhood: the Cordovas, the Flanagans and the Eckerts. The Flanagans had six kids and we immediately connected with them. The youngest was a boy the same age as my brothers, and then there were two girls a little older than me and then the three older boys.

The Flanagan family lived two doors down from us on an adjacent street in the exact same model of house that we had, but there was one major difference: games, both indoor and outdoor, were a central part of this family. Downstairs in the furnace room where in my house we kept the washing machine, a few tools and any odds and ends that couldn't fit anywhere else in the house, the Flanagans had a wall of shelves that housed more board games than I had ever seen in one place except the toy store. They had all the usual games, Monopoly, Parcheesi and Sorry, but they also had some I had never seen like Smess. And all the games had all the pieces!

Their outdoor "playground" was the awe of the neighborhood. The large rectangle yard had a sidewalk down the center. On one side was a bike rack that looked like one you would find in front of a store for people to lock their bikes. It had at least 10 bikes on it—one for each member of the family and a few extra. Behind the bikes sat a sandbox and a swing set. The other side of the yard, just dirt from so much running around on it, had a basketball hoop and a volleyball net.

It was not unusual to see Mr. and Mrs. Flanagan out playing volleyball, basketball or other outdoor games with their family. The neighborhood kids were always welcome and encouraged to join in. Their yard was the hub of activity whether that was playing games inside or outside.

Five years after we moved to Northglenn, a gas leak in the sewer lines changed our lives. Forty-one families, including the Flanagans, were forced to leave and they were never able to return. In one moment our friends and all their games vanished from the neighborhood.

We tried to stay connected, but that special bond that can only happen when you live close to someone eventually faded and we all lost touch.

Fate stepped in five years later when I went off to college and Cindy Flanagan called to invite me to a party (you can read the full story in the Chuck & Eddie's Sister essay). Her older brother Rich was there and following the party we started dating, and when we got married, I officially became a Flanagan. My friends were now my family, and their parents my in-laws. It felt surreal to now be part of both worlds.

The roots of my side of the family (the Stephen side) stretched back to New York City and the Flanagan side to a farm in a small town in Kansas. It became apparent to me early on the different dynamics of family get-togethers, both good, just different.

A Stephen clan function involved the kids entertaining themselves and the adults sitting around, enjoying drinks and lots of loud conversations as everyone talked over one another. The Flanagans started out with the conversation (at a much lower decibel) and then inevitably someone would say, "Who wants to play a game?" If the weather was nice, the games were outside, if not, out came the board games. This is where they sprung to life and their competitive spirits emerged.

Because he had a five-year-old son when I met him, Rich already had a start on his game collection. I'd grab one for all of us to play and ask Rich if all the pieces were there. He would look at me as if I were an alien. Of course all the pieces were there.

After playing a game like Candyland, I would toss the cards in the box, scattering them like pick-up sticks. He'd throw me a scowl and then hand me a rubber band. "You need to keep them all together with this."

Oh.

As the years went on, the rules and responsibilities of being a part of a game family became clearer: Pieces get put back in the box as soon as we are done playing. Game pieces do not co-mingle. A Monopoly house cannot double as a Parcheesi piece. Loose cards and play money are always kept together with a rubber band. If the corner of a game box is ripping, get out the tape and fix it immediately.

Time marched on and as our game closet grew so did our family. I knew it was now partially my responsibility to pass on the ways of a gaming family to our three kids. It wasn't fair to leave that all up to Rich. I took my new role in this process seriously and I soon learned there was more to playing games than just putting everything back in the box. Unspoken rules surfaced and became the foundation of all games: Take turns. Be kind. Friendly competition and banter are encouraged. Be present (no texting). Appreciate this time together.

Now, whenever there is a family get-together at our house I don't have to worry. I am confident that when someone says, "Who wants to play a game?" I can go to our fully stocked closet to find a game and I know all the pieces are there, because after all, I am a Flanagan.

Amtrack Express

—It's all about the journey, right?

My husband Rich and I planned to sneak away for the weekend to Colorado's wine country: Grand Junction. This city of 48,000 is nothing spectacular, but the wineries, peach orchards and the Book Cliff Mountains make it a great destination in September. We looked forward to reconnecting while celebrating my birthday, just the two of us—no kids, no work and no worries.

Typically this 300-mile trek takes five hours by car, but this time we were going to be adventurous and try the train. We were scheduled to arrive at 4:08 p.m., still giving us time to enjoy a Friday night on the town.

Visions of luxury trains I had seen in the movies like the *Murder on the Orient Express* fueled my excitement. Even Harry Potter and his clan traveled in luxury on the Hogwarts Express.

I pictured beautiful dining cars decorated in dark wood with wall-to-wall plush carpeting and flirting with Rich while sipping martinis in the classy lounge car while a jazz quartet played in the corner. When we disembarked, he would go first and then lift me from the last step as the steam from the train enveloped us. Then we'd hold hands as we made our way to the station, our undying love propelling us across the station platform.

***

"Your train's delayed about two hours," said the guy through the small booth window. "You won't be leaving until about 11:00."

"The train is late?" I was not ready to accept this.

The booth guy laughed. "This must be your first time on a train. They're always late."

At this point we should have blown the whistle on the train ride and driven to Grand Junction. But no—I wanted my romantic train ride no matter what!

At 12:05 we finally boarded and the train soon pulled out of the station. I watched the platform slowly pass by. My excitement built as the train gained speed. This was going to be… the train slowed down, then stopped.

The conductor came to collect tickets. We handed him ours and asked what was going on.

"I'm not sure," he said. "We share the tracks with Union Pacific, so a lot of times we have to wait for their train to move past and get to another track."

"How long does it usually take?" I asked.

"Fifteen minutes. An hour. Two hours. We never know. But it happens a lot. Enjoy your trip."

At 12:25 we started going again. My stomach grumbled.

"Rich, what do you say we go check out the viewing car and then get something to eat?"

We found the viewing car full of people sitting on comfortable cushioned benches and swivel chairs, looking out the many windows and basking in the light that came through the clear glass ceiling. Maybe my visions of a romantic train ride would come true after all.

The sign on the dining car said “closed.” It was off to the lounge car. Voices grew louder as we approached, as did the stench of stale beer. My jaw dropped as we entered. Where was the dark wood? The plush carpeting? The jazz? The fancy-dressed men and women?

Orange-colored vinyl booths, like you would find in a greasy spoon diner, lined one wall. A group of four 20-somethings occupied the corner booth, each with a beer in their hand. The way they sprawled themselves around the table made it clear they were way beyond their first drink. Their slurred conversation, sprinkled with profanities, filled the space and drowned out my martini-sipping dream.

We approached the guy wearing a circus-looking vest who stood behind the small counter. Our lunch options resembled what you would find at a minor league baseball game.

“I’ll have a hot dog, chips and a beer,” said Rich.

“Make that two,” I chimed in.

With the last beep of the microwave, our lunch was done. We looked around for a place to sit. Oddly enough the table next to the rowdy quartet was available. I looked at Rich, he looked at me and we went back to our own seats. We ate our ballpark fare and gulped down our beers. According to our calculations the new arrival time would be 8:00 p.m.

To fill the hours, we played Scrabble. The word “delay” popped into my head a few times, but I never got the Y. The spectacular mountain views provided some distraction, but after a while, the scenery all started to look the same, especially after a few more unplanned stops.

Since we were going to be on the train longer than expected, we made reservations for a six o’clock dinner. I was excited. We were going to eat in a real dining car. I imagined the candlelit tables, fine wine and filet mignon.

The voice on the PA system announced, “Those passengers with six o’clock dinner reservations can now come to the dining car.”

I grabbed Rich’s hand and pulled him down the aisle. We shared our table with another couple.

The plastic orange flowers in the small glass vase desperately tried to compliment the starkness of the white tablecloths. When I ordered Chardonnay, the waitress brought the bottle to our table, unscrewed the lid and poured me a glass. Our new dinner companions shared with us what life was like as owners of a trash company and a little about one of their adult children who recently got out of jail. It sounded like something off a cable reality show.

Still in my train fantasy, I ordered the prime rib. We continued our small talk. In the background I heard three consecutive beeps and then the waitress appeared with our plates. I stared in amazement at the cuisine before me. A piece of indistinguishable, brown, shriveled-up meat rested on my plate alongside what I thought were some mixed vegetables. We all just stared at it. Even our tablemates, who had a lot of experience with trash, didn't quite know what to make of it.

We passed on dessert and instead were treated to another notorious train stop, adding another 15 minutes to our trip. I looked out the window and watched dark clouds roll in over the mountains.

On the way back to our seats following dinner, we went to see if there were any seats available in the viewing car before the sun went down. It was full of people smart enough not to eat in the dining car.

Rich and I ambled back to our tiny home away from home. We sank into our seats. We were Scrabbled out. Instead we stared out the window, mesmerized by the sound and swaying of the train while yearning for the outside world again. Rain began falling, dampening more than the ground, but I was determined to stay positive and make the best of the situation.

At 9:12, we pulled into the Glenwood Springs station. Only one hour to go, but that was in real time; train time could be anywhere from two hours to two days. The train sat at that station for about 45 minutes, reminding us who was boss.

We made the trek to the viewing car one more time. This time seats were available, but the only view was the rain sliding down the windows in the darkness. I let out a big sigh and we headed back to home base once again.

Emotional and physical exhaustion crept into us. Tears tried escaping but I squashed them with a giggle. Then Rich started to chuckle. My giggle turned to laughter and pretty soon we couldn't control ourselves and we laughed until it hurt.

At 10:30 p.m., I actually started to get excited again. I knew we were about 20 minutes from our destination, 20 minutes until freedom, 20 minutes until… it happened again. The train stopped. I strained to look out the window into the darkness. My eyes focused on the one lone shed lit up by a single streetlight. We had truly entered the Twilight Zone.

"What's going on?" we asked Mr. Conductor when he wandered by.

"Oh, the engineers' shift is up, so they have to bring in new engineers. Union rules." He smiled.

"How are they going to do that out here in the middle of nowhere?" I asked.

"They are driving them in from Grand Junction. Enjoy the rest of your ride."

Grand Junction?

I looked at Rich and we both laughed. But this time they were more maniacal laughs because reality set in. We were prisoners on a train, in some tiny town on the Western Slope of Colorado. For 40 minutes, we waited while they shuffled the engineers around.

At 11:36 p.m., after being on the train for 11.5 hours, we chugged into the Grand Junction station. We grabbed our stuff and headed for the door. We felt bad for those still left on the train heading to California and hoped they would make it there before Christmas.

We stepped off the train. There was no romantic lifting me off the step, no walking hand in hand through the steam coming off the train. Rich and I trudged along, pulling our small suitcases.

As we got in the shuttle to the hotel we looked at each other. No words were needed. It was clear we were both on the same track. We would definitely be renting a car on Sunday to get home.

Together S'more

—It's the little things that matter

Summertime in Colorado brings with it sunshine, farmer's markets, festivals and for my whole family, camping. During a few weekends between June and August, we load up four pop-up campers with supplies; fill up the coolers with food, drinks and ice; cram eight young kids, four teenagers and ten adults into four cars; and head for the mountains.

To say these camping excursions are relaxing is a bit of a stretch. When our caravan rolls in, we not only invade four adjoining campsites, but also the peaceful nature sounds that once inhabited the area.

Now, interspersed with the wind blowing through the trees and the gurgling stream you will hear, "Grandpa! Can we use the walkie-talkies now?"

"Pull straight back in. A little to the left. Right there. Perfect."

"Did you remember to bring firewood?"

"Where's the bathroom?"

The clicking of our pop-up camper cranks add to the symphony of sounds and soon the small rectangle boxes we pulled behind us for miles magically convert into our homes away from home. The camping chairs get unfolded and placed around the fire pit to form a perfect circle.

With the televisions, computers and cell phones left behind, we all take a deep breath of fresh air and fall into the familiar cadence of our camping weekend. The younger kids unlock their imaginations and climb on the rocks and play make-believe amongst the trees; the teens break out the Frisbees, the washer-board game or set up the badminton; and the adults uncork the wine then sit down, talk and decompress.

At night around the campfire is when it all comes together, where we revive the dying art of oral storytelling. One by one, stories of past camping trips bubble up. My nine-year-old niece remembers when she caught the most fish at Chambers Lake. We all reminisce about the trip to Tunnel Campground where the hummingbirds perched on our fingers and hats. We laugh about our pudgy pie contests and try to remember who now possesses the traveling aluminum foil trophy. One of my brothers reminds us that he is still the champion of the universe at the bean bag game after he beat us all at Olive Ridge. The stories flow, one right into another.

Then after marshmallows are toasted, s'mores are eaten and the sun sets behind the mountains, Dad breaks out the guitar and we sing songs around the campfire, some well-known favorites and some made-up.

It is these moments that remind us that it doesn't matter where we are or what we are doing, what matters is that we are all together, creating memories that will last forever.

We are family.

About The Author

Kerrie is the Director of Northern Colorado Writers, a freelance writer and a writing consultant. She is an accomplished freelance writer with articles in the 2011 Guide to Literary Agents, the past three Writers Markets, Writers Digest Magazine and The Writer. She was a frequent contributor at WOW! Women on Writing. She is the co-author of *Write Away: A Year of Musings & Motivations for Writers*.

Her personal essays have appeared in various Chicken Soup for the Soul books. She enjoyed two years as a contributing editor for Journey magazine, worked in PR for the Fort Collins CVB and for various authors and started The Writing Bug blog.

Prior to her writing career, she was an elementary school teacher for 10 years. Seven years ago she combined her love for writing and teaching with her passion for helping other writers and started Northern Colorado Writers. Through classes, workshops, meetings and an annual conference, NCW is able to provide its 200+ members and other writers, the tools, encouragement and information needed to find success.

www.KerrieFlanagan.com

OTHER HOT CHOCOLATE PRESS BOOKS

HTTP://HOTCHOCOLATEPRESS.COM

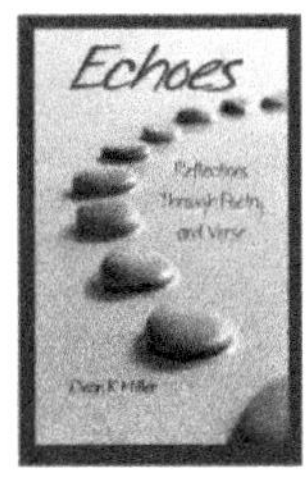

Echoes

Reflections Through Poetry and Verse

https://www.createspace.com/5101546

Save 20% with this code:

EYHLVAZ4

And Then I Smiled

Reflections on a Life

Not Yet Complete

https://www.createspace.com/4644658

Save 20% with the code:

WTFGMW5Y

Write Away

A Year of Musings &

Motivations for Writers

https://www.createspace.com/4800562

Save 20% with the code:

EYHLVAZ4

The Odyssey of a Monk Kindle

Kindle:http://tinyurl.com/n2mhvz9

www.ingramcontent.com/pod-product-compliance
Lightning Source LLC
Chambersburg PA
CBHW071010120726
47910CB00004B/1452

* 9 7 8 0 9 9 1 0 6 2 6 0 7 *